# FUN FACTS ABOUT JAPAN

CHELSEA KONG

PRINTED IN 2024-2026, MADE IN TORONTO, CANADA
ISBN: 978-1-998335-48-0
HARDCOVER ISBN: 978-1-998335-49-7
LIBRARY AND ARCHIVES CANADA

# SUSHI

I LOVE JAPANESE FOOD.
HOW ABOUT YOU?
LET'S EXPLORE JAPAN TOGETHER.
OHAYO おはよう MEANS GOOD MORNING.

# Japan Tour

YOU CAN BOOK A TOUR TO EXPLORE.
LEARN AND PLAN ABOUT JAPAN
AND TASTE AND SEE.

# Japan

**THERE IS SO MUCH MORE TO EXPLORE.**
**A PLACE OF BEAUTY AND FUN.**
**THINGS TO DO FOR ME AND YOU!**

TAKE A WALK AND SEE THE NICE SCENERY IN OSAKA AND KYOTO.

THERE ARE SAND DUNES AND WATERFALLS,
PADDLEBOARDING
AND SNORKELING TOURS.

YOU CAN GO ON HIKES AND ICE TOURS,
MOUNTAINS AND HOT SPRINGS,
ISLANDS AND VOLCANOS.

SEE THE CHERRY BLOSSOM
(SAKURA) IN THEIR SEASON.
HOW BEAUTIFUL THEY BLOOM.

LADIES IN AWASE KIMONOS IN WINTER.
ENJOY THE YUTAKA IN THE SUMMER,
SOFT AND COMFORTABLE TO WEAR.

FESTIVALS IN THE SPRING.
FESTIVALS IN THE FALL.
FESTIVALS IN THE WINTER.
AND THAT'S NOT ALL!

**TREATS, TOYS, SOUVENIRS, FOOD, DRINKS AND MORE TO EXPLORE!**
**DANCES, COSTUME, FLOATS, AND MUSIC.**

TASTY FOOD AND MUCH TO EAT!
I LOVE JAPANESE FOOD.
IT'S A NICE TREAT.

**BARBECUE AND RAMEN,**
**TEPPANYAKI AND UDON,**
**FISH ROE AND MISO.**

OSECHI-RYORI, YAKATORI,
BENTO BOX AND TERRIYAKI.
SIT AND EAT THE NICE FEAST.

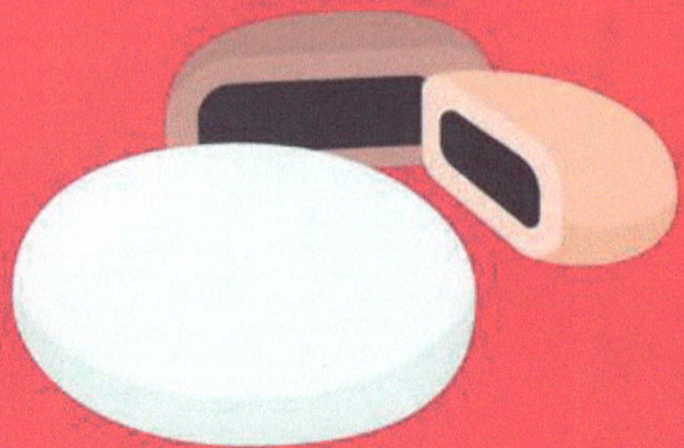

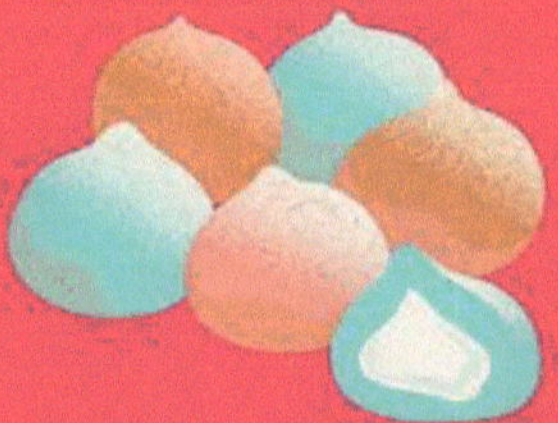

SWEETS ARE SO NICE.
THEY HAVE THEM BOTH BIG AND SMALL.
GET ALL SHAPES, SIZE, AND COLOURS TOO.

NOW TAKE A DRINK,
GOOD ALL YEAR ROUND.
SO MUCH TO BE FOUND!
BUBBLE TEA SO YUMMY!

MATCHA, SAKE, AMAZAKE, FLAVOURED SOY MILK, TAPIOCA DRINKS, POCARI SWEAT, CAPLICO, UMESHU, HOPPY SHOCHU, AND JAPANESE WHISKEY.

THEY SIT AND KNEEL FOR THEIR MEALS AND WHEN THEY DRINK. CAN YOU DO THIS TOO?

ARTS AND CRAFTS ARE SO FUN.
LEARN TO MAKE THEM ONE BY ONE!
PAPER, FABRIC, CLAY, AND GLASS.

**FANS, PAINTINGS, WOOD, AND STONE.**
**ANIME AND MANGA, MOVIES AND GAMES.**
**FUROSHIKI (FOLDING CLOTH) TOO.**

ORIGAMI FOLDS BOTH BIG AND SMALL.
ALL DIFFERENT ONES AND SO MUCH FUN!
BOTH ANIMALS AND THINGS TOO.

**KIRIGAMI, (ONE CUT PAPER) AMIGURUMI, TEMARI, GYOTAKU, BYOBU, MAKI-EK, SAMURAI MASKS, AND NETSUKE.**

STENCIL AND BOOKBINDING COLLAGE, CALLIGRAPHY, POUCHES, BAGS, CERAMIC, EMBROIDERY, TEAPOTS, AND MORE.

DON'T FORGET LAQUEWARE, METAL WORK,
BAMBOO, TEXTILES, STONE,
PRECIOUS STONES, AND SILK.

**YOU WILL FIND THE RED-CROWNED CRANE, USSURI BLACK BEAR, STELLAR'S SEA LION, POND TURTLE, AND GREEN PHEASANT.**

SEE THE GIANT SALAMANDER, SIKA DEER, MACAQUE, DUGONG AND AMAMI RABBIT.

SHIBA INU IS A JAPANESE HUNTING DOG.
SMALL, SPIRITED, AND GOOD IN NATURE.

THERE ARE INDOOR LANTERNS (ANDON)
AND OUTDOOR LANTERNS (TORO).
BOTH BEAUTIFUL AND BRIGHT.

THERE PAPER AND BUCKET LANTERNS (CHOUCHIN) ARE A GREAT DELIGHT! AND THEY MAKE A PERFECT LIGHT IN THE NIGHT.

SPORTS ARE FUN TO SEE AND GREAT TOO. THERE ARE TRADITIONAL SPORTS LIKE KARATE, AIKIDO, KENDO, JUDO, AND SUMO WRESTLING.

COME SEE TOKYO STATION, SKYTREE, TOWER, NAKANO BROADWAY, HYAKUDEN KAIDEN AT HOTEL GAJOEN, IMPERIAL PALACE, AND THE NATIONAL MUSEUM.

HAVE FUN AT GASHAPON DEPARTMENT STORE IKEBUKURO, LIFE-SIZED UNICORN GUNDAM STATUE IN ODAIBA, DOME CITY, AND NAKAMISE SHOPPING STREET.

# ARIGATO
ありがとう

**ARIGATO MEANS THANK YOU.**
**SAYONARA さようなら IS GOODBYE.**
**OTSUKARESAMA DESHITA お疲れ様でした**
**IS THE FORMAL WAY TO SAY GOODBYE.**

# References


JAPAN HORIZON, 2024, "TOP 5 TRADITIONAL SPORTS IN JAPAN: SUMO AND 4 OTHERS"
JAPAN HORIZON, 2024
HTTPS://JAPANHORIZON.COM/5-TRADITIONAL-SPORTS-JAPAN/

WORLDATLAS, 2024
"ANIMALS NATIVE TO JAPAN"
WORLDATLAS, 2024
HTTPS://WWW.WORLDATLAS.COM/ARTICLES/ANIMALS-NATIVE-TO-JAPAN.HTML

TSUNAGU JAPAN, "50 BEST THINGS TO DO IN TOKYO (2024 EDITION)"
TSUNAGU JAPAN
HTTPS://WWW.TSUNAGUJAPAN.COM/50-THINGS-TO-DO-IN-TOKYO-TW/

# Message from the Author

Thank you for reading this book. I hope you can leave a nice review to encourage me to write more books to teach children and adults. It is a fun place to travel and I enjoy writing this book. I enjoy sharing what I learned about Japan. I would love to visit there. They are one of the most famous places to travel. Other places you should visit are Shibuya Scramble Crossing, Go Kart Racing in Akihabara, Metropolitan government building observatories, Ghibli Museum, Hama-rikyu Gardens, Yanesen Area, Tokyo Bay Yakatabune Night Cruise, and Sumida Hokusai Museum. May you enjoy Japan!

# OTHER PRODUCTS

Knowing God
How to Hear God's Voice
New Life in Jesus
Loving Israel
God's Gifts/Spiritual Talents
Meeting God
Word Power
Fruit of the Spirit
The Tabernacle
Bride for Jesus
A Life of Prayer
Live Free
Who am I in Jesus
Walk in Love
God's Favor
Man of God
Woman of God
How to Use Money
God's Wisdom
Fasting
See Jerusalem and Bethany
First Fruit Offering
Feast of Trumpets
Day of Atonement
Feast of Tabernacles
Counting the Omer
Festival of Lights
Glory, Presence, and Holy Spirit
Live in God's Presence
Pentecost
See Galilee, Nazareth, and Tiberias
Hear God Speak
Knowing Jesus
Knowing Holy Spirit
A Healthy Life and Healthy Life Work Book
Smokey the Cat
Passover Unleavened Bread
Resurrection Life
The Blessing
Revival
Chelsea Learns Hebrew
Thanksgiving
Give Thanks
Jesus Birth
Loving Jesus: Bride and Groom
Proverbs 31 Woman

# OTHER PRODUCTS

ABC of People in the Bible
Colours in the Bible
Breakthroughs
Open Doors
The Seven Spirits of God
Numbers in the Bible
Aglee the Eagle
An Eagle's Life
Chelsea Learns Numbers in Hebrew
ABC's of Faith
Feast of Purim
A Royal Life
Family Day
Family Blessings
Chinese New Year
Loving Jesus for Children
Worship
Pandas
Canada
Celia's Birthday
Animal Stories
Eagles
Fun in West Caribbean
Courtroom of God
Fun in Yellowknife
Windsor
Tecumseh
Fragrances in the Bible
Fun in Alberta

**Coming soon**

Fun in Yellowknife
Canada's Government
Creative Arts
A Payroll Career
Fun in Labrador

# OTHER PRODUCTS

Knowing God
How to Hear God's Voice
New Life in Jesus
Loving Israel
God's Gifts/Spiritual Talents
Meeting God
Word Power
Fruit of the Spirit
The Tabernacle
Bride for Jesus
A Life of Prayer
Live Free
Who am I in Jesus
Walk in Love
God's Favor
Man of God
Woman of God
How to Use Money
God's Wisdom
Fasting
See Jerusalem and Bethany
First Fruit Offering
Feast of Trumpets
Day of Atonement
Feast of Tabernacles
Counting the Omer
Festival of Lights
Glory, Presence, and Holy Spirit
Live in God's Presence
Pentecost
See Galilee, Nazareth, and Tiberias
Hear God Speak
Knowing Jesus
Knowing Holy Spirit
A Healthy Life and Healthy Life Work Book
Smokey the Cat
Passover Unleavened Bread
Resurrection Life
The Blessing
Revival
Chelsea Learns Hebrew
Thanksgiving
Give Thanks
Jesus Birth
Loving Jesus: Bride and Groom
Proverbs 31 Woman

# OTHER PRODUCTS

ABC of People in the Bible
Colours in the Bible
Breakthroughs
Open Doors
The Seven Spirits of God
Numbers in the Bible
Aglee the Eagle
An Eagle's Life
Chelsea Learns Numbers in Hebrew
ABC's of Faith
Feast of Purim
A Royal Life
Family Day
Family Blessings
Chinese New Year
Loving Jesus for Children
Worship
Pandas
Canada
Celia's Birthday
Animal Stories
Eagles
Fun in West Caribbean
Courtroom of God
Fun in Yellowknife
Windsor
Tecumseh
Fragrances in the Bible
Fun in Alberta

**Coming soon**

Fun in Yellowknife
Canada's Government
Creative Arts
A Payroll Career
Fun in Labrador

# OTHER PRODUCTS

**Devotionals**

31 Day Devotional

**Inspirational/Other**

Chelsea's Psalms and Poems

Your Daily Meal: Chelsea's Photo Album

Chelsea's Psalms and Poems2

Travel West Caribbean

Chelsea's Recipes

Chelsea's Psalms and Poems3

Travel to Alberta

**Puzzle Books**

Biblical Puzzle Book Vol 1-5

Bible Puzzles for Young Children Book 1-3

Biblical Puzzle for Children Books 1-5

Chelsea's Bible Puzzles

# OTHER PRODUCTS

**Teaching Series**

How to Hear God's Voice Teaching Guide & Audio Book

Relationship with God, Jesus, Holy Spirit Guide

Knowing God, Jesus, Holy Spirit Guide & Audio Book

Flowing in the Prophetic

Teaching (Non-Sale on my website)

Purim

Passover

Resurrection

**Coming soon**

Chelsea's Psalms and Poems4

Travel Yellowknife

# BOOK REVIEWS

More books on Amazon, Kobo, and Barnes and Noble,
Smashwords, and IngramSpark.
https://chelseak532002550.wordpress.com/

More books on Amazon, Kobo, and Barnes and Noble,
Smashwords, and IngramSpark.
https://www.amazon.com/author/chelseakong

Please leave a review and share with friends to help the author continue to write more books to reach more readers. Thank you so much for your support.

Review!

# About CHELSEA KONG

She is a writer, creative arts and digital media artist, skilled administration and certified PCP (Payroll Compliance Professional), and podcaster. She is working on her management certificate in Payroll. Chelsea also served in a variety of roles, from audiovisual, photography, to assisting on the worship team, and ministry team. She also has a passion for families being united.

Chelsea has been a guest on Unity Live Radio, The Lady Tracey Show, and How to Live for Christ and is highly recommended by a Proud Christian blog. She is also a guest blogger. A few of her books have been featured in YourAuthorHub, etc. She graduated from Hotel and Restaurant Management, Digital Media Arts, Office Administration, Payroll Compliance Professional, and experience working with children. Chelsea lives in Toronto, Canada. She mainly writes children's books, stories, bridal writing, poems, lyrics for songs, words of encouragement, blessings, prayers, and jokes. The author of How to Hear the Voice of God, the Bridal Collection, Knowing God, etc. She also has her own Bible Puzzle books and other inspired products. Her podcast channel is called Chelsea K on Anchor, Spotify, and iTunes.

Please check my website to find out more:
https://chelseak532002550.wordpress.com/

www.ingramcontent.com/pod-product-compliance
Lightning Source LLC
Chambersburg PA
CBHW040023180826
50016CB00014B/74
* 9 7 8 1 9 9 8 3 3 5 4 9 7 *